THE POETRY OF NOBELIUM

The Poetry of Nobelium

Walter the Educator

Silent King Books

SILENT KING BOOKS

SKB

Copyright © 2024 by Walter the Educator

All rights reserved. No part of this book may be reproduced in any manner whatsoever without written permission except in the case of brief quotations embodied in critical articles and reviews.

First Printing, 2024

Disclaimer
This book is a literary work; poems are not about specific persons, locations, situations, and/or circumstances unless mentioned in a historical context. This book is for entertainment and informational purposes only. The author and publisher offer this information without warranties expressed or implied. No matter the grounds, neither the author nor the publisher will be accountable for any losses, injuries, or other damages caused by the reader's use of this book. The use of this book acknowledges an understanding and acceptance of this disclaimer.

"Earning a degree in chemistry changed my life!"
- Walter the Educator

dedicated to all the chemistry lovers, like myself, across the world

NOBELIUM

Nobelium reigns with its atomic glance.

NOBELIUM

Obscure in its essence, rare and refined,

NOBELIUM

A gem of the periodic table, one of a kind.

NOBELIUM

Born in the depths of a nuclear blaze,

NOBELIUM

Where stars forge elements in their cosmic craze,

NOBELIUM

Synthesized by humans, in labs it was made,

NOBELIUM

To unlock the secrets of atoms, its purpose arrayed.

NOBELIUM

Named in honor of Alfred Nobel's fame,

NOBELIUM

A tribute to science, its power and acclaim.

NOBELIUM

With electrons swirling in quantum array,

NOBELIUM

Nobelium's mysteries beckon, night and day.

NOBELIUM

In laboratories clandestine, scientists toil,

NOBELIUM

Manipulating particles with precision and coil.

NOBELIUM

In particle accelerators, beams collide,

NOBELIUM

Creating fleeting moments where new elements abide.

NOBELIUM

Nobelium, elusive, with a fleeting life span,

NOBELIUM

Decays into other elements, part of nature's plan.

NOBELIUM

Yet in its transience lies a story untold,

NOBELIUM

Of discovery and wonder, a saga bold.

NOBELIUM

Its properties obscure, its uses few,

NOBELIUM

Yet Nobelium whispers of breakthroughs anew.

NOBELIUM

Perhaps in its depths, lies a key,

NOBELIUM

To unlock the universe's hidden decree.

NOBELIUM

In the hands of researchers, it finds its purpose,

NOBELIUM

In unraveling mysteries, in scientific circus.

NOBELIUM

A puzzle piece in the grand design,

NOBELIUM

Of the cosmos' secrets, of the mysteries divine.

NOBELIUM

So let us marvel at Nobelium's grace,

NOBELIUM

In the dance of atoms, in the cosmic race.

NOBELIUM

A testament to human ingenuity,

NOBELIUM

And the quest for knowledge, our eternal affinity.

NOBELIUM

Though its name may fade in the annals of time,

NOBELIUM

Nobelium's legacy will forever shine.

NOBELIUM

For in its existence, we find the spark,

NOBELIUM

Of human curiosity, illuminating the dark.

NOBELIUM

So here's to Nobelium, element divine,

NOBELIUM

In the tapestry of atoms, a luminary sign.

NOBELIUM

May its secrets unravel, may its story unfold,

NOBELIUM

In the ever-expanding universe, a tale to behold.

NOBELIUM

ABOUT THE CREATOR

Walter the Educator is one of the pseudonyms for Walter Anderson. Formally educated in Chemistry, Business, and Education, he is an educator, an author, a diverse entrepreneur, and he is the son of a disabled war veteran. "Walter the Educator" shares his time between educating and creating. He holds interests and owns several creative projects that entertain, enlighten, enhance, and educate, hoping to inspire and motivate you.

Follow, find new works, and stay up to date with Walter the Educator™ at WaltertheEducator.com

www.ingramcontent.com/pod-product-compliance
Lightning Source LLC
LaVergne TN
LVHW051922060526
838201LV00060B/4130